The Prayer that God Prays

The Prayer that God Prays

JIM ROSEMERGY

Author of A CLOSER WALK WITH GOD

DeVorss Publications
Camarillo, California

The Prayer that God Prays

Copyright© 2004 by Jim Rosemergy

ISBN: 087516-795-0

Library of Congress Control Number: 2003113780

FIRST EDITION, 2004

DeVorss & Company, Publisher

P.O. Box 1389

Camarillo CA 93011-1389

w w w . d e v o r s s . c o m

Printed in the United States of America

TABLE OF CONTENTS

Have you ever suspected that something was true, but you weren't quite sure? You felt an impulse pushing from the inside. It is one thing to be pushed by others, but it is a totally different experience to be pushed from within.

The idea that you sense is contrary to the accepted beliefs of most people. Who are you to question the "tried and true" that humanity has honed for eons? But then again, you are not actually questioning ancient beliefs; something fresh and new is emerging from within you. At least, it is new to you. You don't have the credentials to challenge the norm, but the new idea seems to hold promise. Maybe it could make a difference in people's lives. It is making a difference in yours.

This impulse was the beginning of the book you are about to read, *The Prayer that God Prays*. You can read the book in one sitting. In fact, I believe the first time the book is read, it should not be put aside until the last page is turned. Then let it rest for a day or two before you slowly and deliberately read each of the chapters again. As you read, ask yourself if you are willing to let the prayer God prays be prayed for you.

INTRODUCTION

Questions are a good beginning. They often challenge us to think and live in new ways. Sometimes another person poses the query. At other times, we ask the question, and, at still other times, the question seems to have a divine origin. It rises in our minds like a flower born in the forest where no flowers have bloomed before. The questions to follow are delicate, tender flowers blooming in the shadows of a forest of beliefs held by humanity for thousands of years.

What if the focus of prayer is not the world and our earthly needs and concerns? Could the purpose of our prayers be to prepare us to hear the prayer God prays? What if prayer is not words, but the way we learn the language of Spirit — silence? What if all prayers have the same answer? Could it be true that God knows our needs before we ask? If this is true, why ask for anything? What if God is not far away, but close at hand — closer than hands and feet and breathing? All of these questions give rise to one grand query. Would the answers implied by these questions change the way we pray?

If prayer is not words, how would we pray? If prayer is not about human problems, what is it about? How do we pray if there is only one answer to any prayer we pray? If God knows our needs before we ask, should we ask anyway? Who is the asking for? If God is closer than our next breath, perhaps our purpose in prayer should be to become aware of the God that is close at hand.

Questions are supposed to lead to answers, but these questions invite confusion and more questions; and yet, they are intriguing. They seem to offer new possibilities, and with all the confusion and fear in the world today, something new might lead us to act in ways that invite healing and the discovery of a common ground that is more than planet Earth. Or perhaps it is easier to dismiss the questions and return to the tried and true. Fear often causes us to seek security in what we know rather than to venture into the unknown to find a new way. Initially, this was my response, but there was one thing that made a difference. The questions seemed to have a divine origin; they were flowers blooming where no flowers had bloomed before. As I became willing to learn answers to the questions, I discovered that it was the Creator who has a prayer to pray.

The Prayer that God Prays

CHAPTER ONE

∽

A Brief History of Prayer

A boy climbed to the roof of his house. At first he moved slowly and cautiously from one side of the peak of the roof to the other, but as time passed, he gained confidence. He was less vigilant, became reckless, and lost his balance. Sliding down the roof, he quickly prayed for help. Abruptly, his fall was stopped. He looked around and said, "Never mind, God, I got caught on a nail."

For millennia, we have prayed this way. When there was a problem, we prayed. When there was no problem or the problem had passed, there was no need for prayer, and therefore no need for God. Prayer and problems, we think, are eternally interwoven. Where would one be without the other? When you see one, you see the other. God is our salvation, the One who snatches us from the jaws of difficulty, disease, and death.

Sliding down a roof can motivate us to pray, but so do a variety of other human challenges. In fact, the focus of most prayer is the human condition. The crops need rain, the body needs to be healed, a decision must be made, or a lost job has to be replaced. We want peace of mind and loving relationships. Every area of human endeavor is held high to the Almighty. We pray for victory in war and forget that young people of the other nation will perish, and for severe weather to miss our community — while giving little thought to surrounding towns and cities. We give thanks to God for delivering our child from injury or death in a car accident and forget that our child's best friend is dead and the parents face the deepest grief known to humankind. Does God deliver one child and not another?

Not only is most prayer about worldly matters, it is often an extension of our ego. We want something, and we want it for ourselves. Even the healing of a family member is often just as much for ourselves as for the other person. The prospect of living without the person is more than we can bear.

Prayers are sometimes bargains with God. We negotiate with the Creator. *God, if you do this for me, I will do this for you.* We beg, we beseech, we affirm, and we intone. Our prayers may be spontaneous cries for help or words memorized by generations of believers. We speak our piece, end our prayer with amen, and fail to pause even for a moment to listen for a reply. Sometimes we are attentive, but our ears are attuned to an answer we have already conceived. Prayer opens doors, we are told, so we stand before the door we know hides the answer we want and impatiently tap our foot because we want our answered prayer, and we want it now.

In ancient times, we brought sacrifices to our deity. We brought food and drink and flowers. We believed that the stone or golden idol absorbed the sustenance from the food for its own nourishment. Some cultures believed that their god demanded human sacrifice. Today, many of these practices seem archaic, but we persist in bringing to God needs we cannot fulfill and challenges we cannot resolve. We bring to God names of people and the names of diseases. We name our problem and want God to do something about it. We pray, but with every word and supplication we assume we know the answer. We often share with our omniscient God what we believe must be.

This is a simplistic history of prayer, but in many ways it accurately portrays our "prayerful" relationship with our Creator. It is no wonder that God has a prayer to pray. It is as if the Almighty has listened long enough. Now it is time for Spirit to speak.

∞

CHAPTER TWO

The Perfect Prayer

Many years ago, a woman brought her 19-year-old daughter to Sunday services at the church where I was the minister. Karen, the daughter, had Down's syndrome. Each Sunday after the service, she greeted me. She hugged me as many people did, but she also kissed me on the forehead and on my cheeks and always said, "I love you, God."

I looked forward to Karen's presence at the services, but I was a little embarrassed by her statement, "I love you, God." I understood how she concluded that I was God. Her mother probably told her that one of the purposes of a Sunday service was to worship God, and since I was the one conducting the service and doing most of the talking, Karen concluded that I was God.

I always remembered Karen and her actions. She was the one who supposedly had diminished mental capacity, and I was the one who was supposed to have above average intelligence, but it took me years to understand what happened when she greeted me after the services.

She believed she was in the presence of God, and yet she did not ask for anything. She did not complain that her father had left her and her mother and ask "God" to do something about it. She did not say, "Look at me. I am not like other people. Can't you make me like them?" Instead, Karen's statement was the perfect prayer. "I love you, God." She thought she was in God's presence, and she asked for nothing. She simply expressed love. If there was anything she wanted from God, it was a loving friendship.

The object of most prayers is the human condition. Something is broken, and it needs to be fixed.

We have tried to get it or fix it and have failed. Now it is time for God to act.

But now, as we prepare to receive the prayer that God prays, let us purify our intent. No longer will our prayers be about the human condition. The prayers we pray will be about our spiritual relationship with God.

What would happen in a human relationship if a person constantly asked you for assistance? "I need your time; I need your money. Please watch my kids while I am gone for the day. Can I borrow your lawn equipment?" Never once did the person indicate that he wanted to get to know you. What kind of relationship would you have with this person? Would friendship be possible? This kind of behavior does not work in human relationships. Could it ever bear fruit in a relationship with God?

The truth is that most prayers ask the Almighty to act on our behalf. But by following Karen's example, our prayer life becomes a loving act that asks to know the Creator. It does not call God to action; it is a pure cry and an open heart calling for a loving relationship, a friendship with the One who made us. Long ago, Abraham called God his friend. This is the relationship that awaits us. Karen taught me that a good beginning is, "I love you, God."

PUT IT TO THE TEST

The ideas in this book will often challenge your thinking, but in each instance, you will be asked to put the ideas and principles to the test. Nothing is to be accepted because it is written or because it seems logical. Even though an idea may be easily accepted by you, put it to the test. And, of course, if you balk at an idea, open your mind and heart to something new. If you read a book and everything you read is old news, there was no reason to read it.

Intellectual confirmation does not change us. Experience is our teacher and that which roots ideas in our souls. For a period of forty days, put aside your human prayers of me and mine. Instead, let your intent in prayer be friendship with God. Pray the perfect prayer. It is a simple prayer, but one we are all called to pray. When our prayers open our hearts to God rather than begging God to give us what we supposedly want, a friendship is forged that is forever. As human beings, we have prayed for many things; today we begin to discover that it is God we truly want.

Every four days, record any experiences or insights you have in response to praying Karen's prayer. As the days progress, pay particular attention to your relationship with your Creator.

DAY 4 _____

_____

_____

_____

DAY 8

....

_____

....

....

DAY 12

....

_____

....

....

DAY 16

....

_____

....

_____

The Perfect Prayer

DAY 20

DAY 24

DAY 28

11

DAY 32

....

_____

....

_____

DAY 36

....

_____

....

_____

DAY 40

....

_____

....

_____

CHAPTER THREE

∞

Prayer Without Words

If you were asked to sign a petition endorsing prayer in public schools, would you sign it? If you were asked to sign a petition upholding the principle of the separation of church and state and therefore banning prayer in public schools, would you sign it? It would be interesting to conduct a survey to determine the percentage of people who would sign either petition. It would also be revealing to know how many people realize that prayer cannot be banned from public schools and that prayer does not become a part of the public school system because particular words are recited during the course of a school day.

For too long, we have limited prayer by thinking of it as words we speak. When I was a child in the public school system and even when I was in college, I would pause and silently pray before every test I took. (It wasn't exactly Karen's prayer.) The constitutional principle of separation of church and state did not stop me from opening myself to the wisdom of God.

If you are a prayerful person and your denomination published a book of prayers, you might buy it and be helped by its contents, but you might also consider that no book can contain a prayer. It depends on what you think prayer is. For eons prayer and words have been woven together in the human psyche. But what if prayer is not words? What if prayer is more than words? What if prayer is an experience of the presence of God?

If for a time, you adopted the idea that prayer is an experience of God's presence, how would this idea change the way you pray? You would realize that prayer cannot be legislated into a school day, nor can it be banned. Children in school could pray at any time by simply opening themselves to a friendship with God. No earthly authority could prevent this friendship or prayerful experience. And, of course, no book can contain a consciousness of God. Only a human being is a vessel for such an experience.

If we embrace this new insight into prayer, it does not necessarily mean we will never again open a prayer book or speak the words of the Lord's Prayer or the great statement of the Jewish faith, "Hear, O Israel, the Lord our God is One Lord." In fact, speaking these words can become more meaningful because they prepare us for the experience of the Presence. No longer do we speak our words, say amen, and go our way. We let what we have called prayer lift us up to wait expectantly, faithfully, and silently for the knowing that our Friend is with us.

This slight shift in emphasis takes us one step closer to the prayer that God prays. When prayer is something we do, we cannot experience God's prayer, but when we do our spiritual work and learn to wait, our relationship with our Creator grows.

Millions of "prayers" must be uttered by human beings every day. Hundreds of prayer practices and techniques are used by devotees of the many religions of the world. Most of these practices and techniques do two things. They focus our attention and lift up our consciousness. Once this work is done, the waiting begins. How else will we hear the prayer that God is praying?

OWN WORK

Here is a prayer practice that balances the words we speak with listening for God's response. First, we pray the perfect prayer by vocally saying or mentally thinking, "I love you, God." Then we ask, "Do You love me?" The question is followed by listening, waiting, and trusting. If the mind drifts and is no longer attentive, we pray the perfect prayer again. Then we ask the question, and wait once more. Do this for twenty minutes a day for a period of seven days.

It is important that we focus as we do this work. Mystics call this recollection. A recollected mind is a mind dwelling in the moment and focused on the prayer practice. In the "Own Work" above, full attention is given to each word that is thought or spoken. When we wait, we are expectant and we watch carefully. It is as if we are looking at a door through which we know our beloved will emerge.

You may intellectually know that God loves you, but this kind of knowing does not transform you or make you attentive to God's prayer. However, when you experience God's love, even in simple ways, an indelible mark is made on your soul. God's love is no longer a belief; it is a reality that no one can take away from you. The person who knows love through experience attuns himself or herself to the voice of God.

CHAPTER FOUR

∽

Learning to Wait

During Jesus' ministry, He gathered with His disciples at Caesarea Philippi, the location of one of the three sources of the River Jordan. Over the sound of water rushing from an underground stream, Jesus asked, "Whom do men say the Son of man is?" And they said, "Some say John the Baptist, others say Elijah, and others Jeremiah or one of the prophets." He said to them, "But whom do you say that I am?" (Matt. 16:13–15)

Jesus' second question stirred Simon Peter, and Peter's answer came from the presence of God within him. He was just as much a listener as the one who spoke. "You are the Christ, the Son of the living God."

Jesus answered him, "Blessed are you, Simon Bar-Jona! For flesh and blood have not revealed this to you, but my Father, who is in heaven." (Matt. 16:17)

Answers can change our lives, but so can questions. Saul, who became Paul, heard a question on the road to Damascus, that changed his life forever. "Saul, Saul, why do you persecute me?" (Acts 9:4)

Let us put aside our quest for answers for a time, and, instead, ask for a question that will stir us. The question does not need to have an answer. We do not need a reply. The question may remain with us for the rest of our lives either as a thorn in our side, as a constant reminder of some value we are to hold dear, or as a message of who we are and why we are here.

Ask for a question that will change you. The question may come immediately, but usually it takes days or weeks before this harbinger of transformation makes itself known. The delay occurs because we must learn to wait and develop the virtue of patience.

A young girl grew up on a farm. From an early age, she was fascinated by windmills. She determined that one day, she would build a windmill on the family farm to harness the energetic winds that blew across the hillside fields. In college, she studied engineering and learned about forces, materials, and mechanical design. She returned home prepared to begin construction. In time she had a beautifully built windmill – but at first the blades did not turn. She needed to adjust them to catch the wind. But still they did not turn – for several days there was no wind. She now knew that the power was in God's hands, hot hers, and she must simply wait and watch for the winds to arrive.

To receive the power of God's love, we must prepare ourselves. We study the principles by which the universe works. We grow clear in our intention and build a life that is ready to welcome Spirit. Then we turn our faces toward God and wait expectantly.

Waiting is the great challenge of the spiritual life. No one has heard the prayer that God prays without first learning how to wait. Remember that most prayer practices focus our minds and lift our consciousness to the place where we wait. The challenge is that our minds drift, memories erupt from our past, and emotions we have buried resurrect themselves. Our thoughts are like butterflies fluttering from flower to flower. We begin to think about the past or to ponder what lies ahead. The power and wonder of the present moment is lost to us because we are in a far country whose name is either past or future.

Do you remember the old water pump in your grandparents' backyard? My grandfather used to pump water from a well for his garden and flowers during the dry season. The water flowed easily as he worked the crooked handle of the pump. Later in the day, I would pump the handle to no avail. It appeared as though the well were dry, but I knew it was not. The pump had to be primed. There was always a bucket of water nearby. I poured the water into the pump and, in a short time, I heard the sound of the rising water.

Prayer is like this. We have our work to do. We prime the pump by pouring in the first water. We lift the handle again and again, and then water rises to help sustain the beauty of the earth. When we speak our prayers, this is priming the pump. We do our work, and then something abundant and refreshing rises up in us, and we are nourished.

Prayer is also like climbing a mountain. It is hard work, but eventually we come to a high meadow where patches of wildflowers bloom. As we pause in this beautiful place and look down the mountain, we see visions we have never seen before. The high meadow is a refreshing place, but it is the summit of the mountain that calls us. We look for the trail, but a mist shrouds the peak, and it is so dense that we cannot find the path. So we wait for a woman to come out of the mist and take us by the hand and lead us. The woman's name is Grace, and it is through her, through grace, that we enter the mist or mystery of God's presence and eventually stand on the summit of the mountain.

Prayer is like this. We have our work to do. We climb to the high meadow, and then we wait. We can venture no farther through our own efforts alone. Through grace, we are guided higher in consciousness until we experience God's presence.

Prayer is also like soaring on the wind. Consider a bird thrusting its mighty wings through the air near a high bluff that faces the prevailing winds. The winds blow, creating an updraft. The bird's effort lifts it from the ground, but suddenly it senses the air current rising up the face of the cliff. The bird spreads its wings and is effortlessly lifted by an unseen presence and force. With effort the bird placed itself in the updraft, but now it rises effortlessly. An unseen force is doing the work.

Prayer is like this. We have our work to do. Through effort, by audibly and mentally speaking our prayers, we draw near to the unseen presence of God. But through our efforts we cannot enter the kingdom of God, so we wait, we stretch out our wings, and we are lifted into higher states of mind and heart. Sometimes the Spirit-wind lifts us into realms beyond the reach of me and mine, of earth and sky, and of sickness and death. We know through experience that the kingdom of God is closer than hands and feet and breathing.

These three images — priming the pump, waiting at the high meadow, and stretching forth our wings — stress the need to do our work in prayer. But it is obvious that the actual experience of the Presence is not something we do; it is God's work.

The great challenge of prayer is waiting. While we wait, the mind drifts down the mountain or back to the world where we are anchored. Three things will bring us through this challenge: persistence, nonresistance, and love. They are our work to do.

Persistence is obvious. Those who fail are the ones who quit. Nothing of consequence is ever accomplished without persistence because the things that truly matter are not easy. In fact, the harder the challenge, the more strength we discover when we accept it.

Nonresistance and love are not so obvious. When we wait, the mind drifts from its focus and returns to worldly and material matters. Feelings emerge that we would rather not experience or that we suppressed in the past. Prayer does the sacred work of uncovering us.

Our approach to these "unwelcome guests" is nonresistance and love. We do not hide from the thoughts or feelings. We do not try to push them away or ignore them the way some people ignore a beggar on the street. Instead, we invite them to "sit with us" and tell us their story. We do not judge them or call them bad or good.

Through nonresistance and love, we embrace parts of ourselves we have shunned, and in doing so, we know ourselves as we have never known ourselves before. We accept ourselves just the way we are. This is love in action.

As you can see, our waiting is a "rest most busy," for through persistence, nonresistance, and love we become focused and able to sense the subtleties of the spirit-wind that lifts us up or to spy Grace emerging from the mist. And it is only on the summit or while resting in the arms of the spirit-wind that we learn the prayer that God is praying.

OWN WORK

Now you understand the need for waiting, and you have some ideas about how to deal with the roving mind. Put these ideas to the test in the coming days as you ask for a question that will stir you. In the past, you may have found it difficult to listen as you asked the question, "Do you love me, God?" Now is the time to take what you have learned about waiting and ask the question again. Then give yourself to this chapter's prayer practice of asking for a question that will stir you.

You will experience many gifts when you put these principles to the test. To know you are God's beloved is moving beyond words. A question such as the one that changed Saul or enlightened Simon Peter will be remembered as a turning point in your life. As a bonus, you will also know the power of patience, persistence, and nonresistance because you learned to wait.

A Personal Experience

I have put this prayer practice of asking for a transforming question to the test. Two questions have come to me that I will never forget. The first was solely for me, a question that can be answered every day of my life and, in fact, many times throughout a day: *Why do you do the things you do?* This question brings me face to face with my motivation. To be conscious of one's intent is a gift for daily living.

The second question, I believe, was and is a gift for the human family. Prior to this moment, I have only shared it verbally. One evening I was reflecting on the poverty of our planet and the many people whose lives are in jeopardy because of famine and drought. In my contemplation, I was asking why this was so. Why are so many people living without adequate food and clean water? In response to my contemplation came a clear question that is gift to the human family: *Why don't you care for one another?* This is the answer, isn't it? When we care for one another rather than fear one another, we will pick our many resources to use in service of the whole human family. And I trust that the first to experience our new consciousness of oneness will be those who are in harm's way.

Ask for a question, dear friend, and Spirit will give you a gift that stirs you and turns you around, so you can see the world clearly.

∽

CHAPTER FIVE

Answered Prayer

The guidance seems clear. "Ask and it will be given you, seek and you will find, knock and it will be opened to you." (Matt. 7:7) Likewise, we are told, "Ask, believing that you have received it, and it will be yours." (Mark 11:24) Obviously, we are encouraged to ask, but it is also written that God knows our needs *before* we ask. If this is true, what's the asking for? It must be for us, not for God. Perhaps asking makes us more receptive — but receptive to what?

When we grow from childhood into adulthood, our wants and desires change, so we ask for different things. Children ask for toys; adults want things that they think provide security or are symbols of success.

When we grow spiritually, what we ask for changes just as when we grow from childhood to adulthood. As we mature spiritually, what we yearn for changes. There comes a time when what we want is just what God is offering us. Part of humanity's challenge is that our Creator is offering us something of great value, but we continue to believe that earthly things can fulfill us.

Humanity tends to believe that God has many things for us. This is not true. God offers us something called the kingdom. "It is the Father's good pleasure to give you the kingdom." (Luke 12:32) Jesus supported the importance of this gift when He said, "Seek first the kingdom of God and His righteousness, and all these things shall be added unto you." (Matt. 6:33) These two statements hold great promise.

Our spiritual lives deepen when we ask for the kingdom rather than earthly things. Remember, the promise is that if we seek the kingdom, all the other things we need will be provided. This kingdom is the pearl of great price, for we will sell everything in order to have it.

Nearly thirty years ago, I saw the possibilities within Jesus' statement, "Seek first the kingdom," and I decided to make it the foundation of my spiritual life and my relationship with God. At the time, I did not know that the promise was true, but I was willing to put it to the test. I built my life on this idea with the hope that it was a rock, and not just shifting sand. Now I know from experience that there is nothing to fear. The promise is true; it is being fulfilled in my life and is a foundation large and strong enough to hold the dreams and hopes of every human being.

We can ask for many things, but as we mature spiritually, the time comes when we ask for one thing — the kingdom of God. Receiving or becoming aware of the kingdom is the answer to our prayer. Our asking and God's giving are finally aligned. Interior joy and peace that bypass understanding are now natural.

Many people are unaware of the nature of the kingdom. They think of it as the dwelling place of God and a place where they will live one day. But here is my challenge to you. Put aside your preconceived ideas about the kingdom of God. Remember, this is God's kingdom, and it is likely that our human minds have not yet fully grasped its nature and wonder. Simply ask for the kingdom. Don't let your earthly desires and needs enter this time of communion with God. Ask for the kingdom, and allow its nature to be revealed to you as you receive it. In this way, your knowing is based on experience rather than the opinions of others. When it comes to the kingdom, God is a better teacher than the most learned human being.

OWN WORK

Ask for the kingdom and journal about your experiences. Write what you discover about the nature of the kingdom of heaven or the kingdom of God.

CHAPTER SIX

∞

The Language of Spirit

Silence is thought to be the absence of sound. It seems empty, a void waiting to be filled with a word or a song. But long ago it was discovered that silence is the presence of God. St. Augustine said that "The best thing to be said about God is silence." This is why when we are silent, we draw near to God. My wife rediscovered this truth in her own prayer and meditation time when this thought filled her mind, "Silence is not the absence of sound; it is the presence of God."

Two people once sat together in silence. For hours neither spoke a word, but each was attentive to the other. As the evening drew to a close, they stood and said to one another that it was one of the most profound evenings of their lives. Only the silence that transcends the absence of sound can grant such a moving experience.

In the 6th century, St. Isaac of Spoleto said, "Silence is the language of the centuries to come." The time St. Isaac foretold is now. The prayer that God prays is to be made known, but before we can learn the prayer, we must learn the language of silence. For minds and ears accustomed to thoughts and sounds, this new language seems unknowable, for it is beyond sound, thought, feeling, and image. For so long these four messengers have brought us our world and, in fact, our lives. Our constant attention to them makes learning God's language a challenge. But because you are reading this book, you must be one destined to learn the language.

We learn a new language best when we are immersed in it. We become comfortable hearing the sounds of it around us. We can travel to the country where the language is spoken, or we can take an immersion class where the teacher speaks almost exclusively in the language we are learning. This method is frustrating, but we quickly learn that clinging to our native tongue does not acquaint us with the new language.

Here is a good way to begin to learn the language of Spirit. Do two things as quickly as you can. First, spend a day alone in silence. Do not speak, and insure that you are in a place where no one will speak to you. In this way, you initially become familiar not with silence, but with your own interior thoughts, feelings, and images. This is important, for this practice will acquaint you with someone you may not know as well as you think — yourself. Thoughts, feelings, and images will fill your day of silence. You will discover what you value and what you typically think about during a day. The mind is habitual in its thinking, so it will give attention to what you have been giving attention to for years.

Don't resist the thoughts, feelings, and images. Watch them as you would observe a child at play. Know thyself. Discover your interior world. This is the beginning of learning the language of Spirit. Next, deepen this experience with the second practice, which is an extension of the first. Spend three days in silence. Take no books or tapes with you, only a pen and notebook to record your experience. Embrace all feelings and images as well as thoughts. Sit quietly, and you will first discover that the silence is filled with you and your concerns. But eventually, the natural state of the mind will descend upon you — stillness, silence, and the now. Like a still body of water, your mind will reflect the heavens above.

Our imagination, thinking and feeling natures were not conceived to be our servants. They were made to be avenues of God's expression. In fact, any or all of our faculties of thought, feeling, and imagination can be the "mouthpiece of God's prayer." Sometimes what we hear, know, feel, or see is for us alone. At other times, it is for the whole world.

Consider your life for a moment. How long do you usually go before you speak or hear sounds of voices other than the birds of the air or crickets in the night? Let us not be surprised that a day or two or three of silence is as much as we can bear. Remember, at this time, the unbearable is not the silence, but ourselves. We have not yet experienced ourselves. We are habitually in the company of other people and other voices. However, the day is coming when there is first us and God, and then, through the gift of grace, only God. For people unaccustomed to silence and consequently to themselves, the most difficult part of learning the language of Spirit is accepting ourselves as we are. It is this lack of self-acceptance that prevents us from accepting other people as they are and from accepting conditions in the world that we cannot change.

During your days of silence, form an image of a great banquet in which your thoughts, feelings, and images are the honored guests. When one of these guests rises to speak, listen carefully. Encourage the guest to tell its story. If it weeps, weep with it, for any hurt will be your own. Make no judgment of what is said or felt. Respond to any thoughts, feelings, or images only with, "Thank you, I am glad you are here and that you stood to speak."

From this simple exercise comes peace. You will become acquainted with parts of yourself that you have not seen for years. Stillness will descend upon you like a dove and prepare you for the prayer that God prays. When you can bear the silence and call it a friend, you can hear God's prayer.

CHAPTER SEVEN

The Prayer

Prayer is now redefined. It is an experience of the presence and power that God is. We can prepare for the experience, but we cannot make it happen. It comes to us through grace, a gift of God's love. Hundreds of prayer practices are used by the human family, but what we have called prayer is actually our preparation for God's work. Our new definition of prayer is that it is what God does, not what we do. We prime the pump, ascend the mountain and wait at the high meadow, and spread our wings, but Spirit is the one who prays.

The prayer that is God's work is not simply an experience that comes and goes. Every experience makes an indelible mark on our souls. In some way it changes us. It strips away the coarse stone and begins to reveal the image of God that rests within each of us. Our lives are transformed as God prays.

I used to say that prayer was the most important thing in my life, but I realize I was referring to my prayer practices. Now I see this differently; it is God praying that is most important. The experience touches me, moves me, and remakes me.

The Bible is more than a history of religious thought, of the Hebrew people, of Christianity, or Jesus' life and teachings. It is a record of humanity's encounters with the Creator. In truth, all sacred literature records these sacred meetings. Each encounter is God praying, for the experience does not come because of the actions of a human being, but because of the mysterious activity of Spirit.

I remember when the idea of God praying first entered my consciousness. It confused me; it pushed me from within just like the questions at the beginning of this book. I could hardly fathom the idea of God praying. To make matters more mysterious, this statement, given to me by Spirit, made me shake my head: *Your life is a prayer that I am praying.* I personalized it and often began my prayer practice with the statement: *My life is a prayer that God is praying.* But I did not really know what that meant. And yet, the idea of my life being a prayer that God prays touched some unknown part of me.

As I continued to ponder the concept, it took years of quiet contemplation and reflection before I began to understand the meaning. My hope is that you will begin to grasp the idea more quickly than I did. This book was written to inspire your understanding and willingness to open yourself to the possibility that your life is a prayer that God is praying.

Can you see that it is these encounters with God that transform us? It happened to Simon Peter at Caesarea Philippi, Saul on the road to Damascus, Moses at the burning bush, Buddha sitting beneath the Bodhi tree, and Mohammed in a cave on Mt. Hira on what the Muslems call the night of power. These, of course, were extraordinary people, but they were extraordinary because of their experience of the presence of God. In their own ways, each sought the kingdom, and eventually the transformation took place.

We may never lead spiritual movements like the people listed above, but every experience of the Presence changes us in a deep way. A creativity will surge from within us as we sense ourselves connected to a fount of knowing. We will experience a peace that does not depend on outer conditions. In fact, we will be peaceful under stressful conditions that make most people falter. Usually, we first see the Divine in nature, but eventually we will see the Presence in other people, even those who appear most human or barely human. As God continues to pray, our family and friends will note a joy and gentleness about us. Our relationship with others becomes genuinely loving because we need nothing from them when we know ourselves to be whole.

One day my wife and I went to a friend's house to pick up an item. Nancy went inside to get it, and I remained outside in the car. I looked out the window at several roses that were planted by the driveway, and suddenly I began to cry. A wave of emotion washed through me, and then it was gone. When Nancy returned to the car, she saw my reddened eyes and asked what was wrong. I said, "Nothing. God just passed by."

Intellectually, I know God does not pass by. My God is omnipresent and therefore does not "go" anywhere. When you are everywhere equally present, there is no place to go. However, for a brief time I became aware of God's presence, and the experience overwhelmed me. In some way I may never understand, I was changed. In that moment, my life was a prayer that God prayed. Silence and stillness continue to be our companions because they are most like

God. Our prayer practices are no longer about ourselves and the world. They prepare us to "hear" the
prayer that God is praying, to experience the Presence.
God's prayer is life, and the prayer is constantly being
prayed. Each time one of us hears it, the world is
closer to transformation. We hear it as silence, we
sense it as stillness, and we know it is God's prayer
because our lives are changed.

FRUITS OF SPIRIT EXPERIMENT

In the spring of 1992, Nancy and I initiated a prayer
experiment that we called "Fruits of Spirit." The
experiment began on Easter Sunday, April 19th and
ended on July 11, 1992. The prayer practice of the
participants was based on Gal. 5:22–23. *But the fruit
of the Spirit is love, joy, peace, patience, kindness, goodness, faithfulness, gentleness, self-control...* Each partici-
pant in the experiment worked with the following
ideas: *May I bear your fruits of love, joy, peace, patience,*

kindness, goodness, faithfulness, gentleness, and self-control. In addition, each person was to note not only changes that took place in his or her interior life, but also changes that took place in the world.

Each person was asked to pray for twenty minutes each day. The average number of days people prayed was nearly six days out of each week, and the preferred time for their prayer practice was early morning.

The results were noticeable with participants recognizing specific improvements in their lives such as:

- Less anxiety at work
- Fewer aches and pain
- Improved creativity
- Greater awareness of beauty in life
- Learned to receive love
- Expanded their ability to trust
- Started speaking more forthrightly
- Became more involved in life
- Fewer emotional responses to angry people

THE PRAYER THAT GOD PRAYS

- More patience in traffic
- Lost twenty pounds
- Became more accepting of their own mistakes
- Greater courage to stretch beyond their comfort zone
- God seemed closer, less distant

This is the height of prayer. First, there is stillness and silence, and then through grace, our lives are changed. In the past we would have said that we prayed, but now we say we simply initiated our prayer practice and waited for God's response. It may have been a sense of peace or profound joy that settled upon us, an idea that came to us, or an insight into some situation in our lives. Perhaps a memory of some past hurt surfaced and was healed and released. Maybe we realized it was time to forgive our father or mother or child. The possibilities are infinite, and each one of them is God praying. It is an experience of the presence and power of God.

The good news is that often the experience changes us and becomes our life. This is why I say that our lives are the prayers that God is praying, for every experience of God transforms us and becomes a part of our souls and our lives.

THE STILL POOL

Through the years, I have given attention to the practicality of prayer practices. Do they make a difference? Are they helpful? How are the results made manifest in our lives? In fact, the greater, more far-reaching question is, do they manifest themselves *as* our lives?

Imagine a placid pool of water into which a small stone is dropped. Immediately, ever-expanding concentric circles radiate out from the place where the stone entered the water. The stone is our simple prayerful attitude. The ripples are prayer becoming life. They are God praying our lives into being. This is the incredible life that is lived when our purpose is knowing and experiencing the Presence.

The center of the circles is our experience of God's presence. It is pure silence — a consciousness of Spirit. Consciousness tends to manifest itself, and the extraordinary result is that a consciousness of God will manifest itself as an ever deepening spiritual life and an ever increasing creative and practical life of service to the human family.

The journey from silence to our lives, from the center of the circle to the most distant circumference, passes through various stages. First, we may experience Spirit pouring Itself through one of our faculties. It may manifest Itself as a thought. Many emerging mystics have been mystified when the two words, *only God*, were etched in their minds. At other times, a feeling may permeate one's being. Peace descends on us, for Spirit is pouring Itself through our feeling nature. Our God may also enter our imagination as we receive guidance through a dream, a waking vision, or an image that makes its home in our mind.

I remember one counseling session in which the other person and I paused for a time of stillness and silence. As we waited together, an image entered my mind that I have never forgotten. I saw a golden chalice overflowing with light shaped like tiny hearts. This image carried the message of love, light, and divine sustenance and abundance. It was a blessing to me, and I trust that this consciousness of God was also a blessing to the other person.

Sometimes an experience of the Presence will manifest Itself as an idea. Please note that thoughts, feelings, and images, as well as ideas, are all parts of our interior world. At this point, there has been no impact on our outer world — but it is coming. Thoughts, feelings, and images make indelible marks on our souls. Through them we know that God is real and life has meaning. By acting on them, we make them manifest in our daily lives.

God's prayer does not stop within our souls. It also transforms our bodies. This is how healings take place. The movement from the silence extends from our interior world into our bodies and then into our relationships with other people. Our professional lives are affected. Our souls are sensitized, so we can recognize opportunities. In fact, it is probably true to say that opportunities for spiritual growth as well as wholesome living come to us every day, but we are not aware of them. One of the blessings of an experience of God's presence is that we become sensitized to the subtleties of daily life and the movement of Spirit within us and the world in which we live.

This is prayer becoming life. It begins with silence, and the ripples continue to radiate through our lives and to become our lives. This is when the meaning of the statement *My life is a prayer that God is praying* begins to dawn in us. In fact, I believe the idea of God's prayer, and specifically this statement *My life is a prayer that God is praying,* came to me as a ripple in the pond. It was God at work. At first the idea was a wave that rolled over me and staggered my thoughts about prayer. Now the wave has settled into gentle ripples that caress and comfort me.

Sit and wait in silence beside the still pond, and cast your prayer stone into the water. You must not be dismayed as the waves wash over you. They will cleanse you, and the prayer that God prays will become your life.

CHAPTER EIGHT

Prayer Practices

Preparing Yourself for the Prayer that God Prays

Prayer and problems were once woven together into the fabric of the human consciousness. Now let us weave a new tapestry in which prayer and friendship with God are central for each of us. Prayer and words were once woven together in our consciousness. How could there be one without the other? Now we see that prayer and silence are the interwoven threads of the new tapestry.

The following steps present a summary of the prayer practices introduced in *The Prayer that God*

Prays. Be gentle with yourself as you work with them. They will prepare you to "hear" the prayer God has wanted to pray ever since you were created.

FIRST STEP

Put aside your earthly concerns and ask for a loving relationship with God. Pray the perfect prayer that Karen taught with her life: *I love you, God.* Mentally or verbally speak these words. They are a good beginning, for they purify your intent and desire. Take the first step on three consecutive days. Whenever your mind turns to God during these days, employ this prayer practice. Record your experience in the space provided here.

Prayer Practices

DAY 1 _____

_____

_____

_____

DAY 2 _____

_____

_____

_____

DAY 3 _____

_____

_____

_____

SECOND STEP

Continue to pray the perfect prayer and add the question, "Do You love me?" Do this for four days. During this time, your primary responsibility is openness and receptivity. You are waiting, listening, trusting, and inviting grace to come into your life. In the space provided, record your experience.

DAY 1 _____

_____

_____

_____

Prayer Practices

DAY 2 ....

_____

_____

_____

DAY 3 ....

_____

_____

_____

DAY 4 ....

_____

_____

_____

Things to Remember

- Prayer practices require that you learn to wait.

- The power of persistence. You are on a spiritual journey. There is no failure, only delays when you quit, and you quit only for a time. The impulse to return to God always remains within you.

- The power of nonresistance. The thoughts, feelings, and images that emerge while you wait are not to be put aside or shunned. They bring opportunities for cleansing and understanding.

- The power of love. The thoughts, feelings, and images that emerge while you wait are not to be judged as bad or good. Each "unwelcome" guest is invited to sit with you and tell its story. These are honored guests bearing messages that teach us to love.

- To know these guests is to know ourselves, for only those who know themselves can hear the prayer that God prays.

THIRD STEP

As a part of each day's prayer practice, ask for a question that stirs you. Ask until the question is given, and write the question you received in the space below. This question does not need to have an answer and may become a companion for your life.

MY QUESTION:

FOURTH STEP

In response to Jesus' statement, *Seek first the kingdom*, ask for the kingdom and allow its nature to be revealed to you. Record the insights that come to you. Please note that the nature of the kingdom will most likely be revealed to you over the course of your life. This will be a page you will return to again and again.

FIFTH STEP

Learn the language of Spirit. As soon as you can, give yourself the gift of a day of silence as outlined in Chapter 6, and then follow it as quickly as you can with the three-day prayer practice using the ideas in that chapter titled "The Language of Spirit." During these days of silence, record your experiences and the insights that come to you. Journaling pages are provided at the end of this book.

SIXTH STEP

Your prayer practices invite God to transform your life. For a period of 40 days, hold in mind as firmly as you can the following statement: *My life is a prayer that God is praying.* During this time, become sensitive to the changes that will inevitably take place in your life. Ideas will come. New opportunities will be recognized. You will experience a new strength in the face of difficulties and an enhanced ability to persist. You will be more sensitive to and accepting of other people because you are more sensitive to and accepting of yourself.

Your life is now in God's hands. You are God's responsibility. Your responsibility is to prime the pump, spread your wings, climb to the high meadow, and wait. Prayer is no longer about the world or primarily words. Prayer is an experience of the presence of God, and it is becoming life — your life.

SILENCE JOURNAL

_____

_____

_____

_____

_____

_____

_____

_____

_____

_____

_____

_____

_____

_____